Embrace Your Features
Published by Christina Testut Publishing

Text copyright © Christina Testut
Illustrations copyright © Ayan Mansoori
All rights reserved.

Typography by Kateryna Barbina.
Edited by Emily Dick and Stephanie Cullen.

Reproduction of this book in any manner, in whole or in part, without the publisher's written permission is prohibited.

EmbraceYourFeatures@gmail.com

Print Paperback ISBN:978-1-7390298-5-2
Print Hardcover ISBN: 978-1-7390298-6-9
eBook ISBN: 978-1-7390298-7-6

Second print edition.

This book is dedicated to all my past, present, and future students. To my children, Emily and Christopher. May you always embrace your features and know that you are worthy and enough just as you are.

When you look in the mirror, what do you see? Maybe skin, eyes, a nose — but we don't all look the same, do we?

That's because we all have FEATURES!
Those are the things that that make us look unique.

The part of you that the world sees is just ONE part of who you are.

No matter what you look like, there is so much more to you than how you appear. You are also kind and smart!

You may wonder why you don't look the same as those you see on the screen.

We can forget that we are worthy of being loved just exactly as we are.

When we listen to
what others tell us how we should be,
we think of our human uniqueness as FLAWS.

But they are NOT defects
or imperfections at all.

Your eyes let you see the world from your point of view. They are a gift because no one else sees through them but you.

Wavy or frizzy, short or long, with braids, locs, or let loose — it doesn't matter if your hair is curly or straight.

Any style you pick, you can't go wrong.

You might have a little or a lot of hair. It might be blond, brown, red, or jet-black. Whatever you have, you wear it best!

Skin comes in all kinds of colors — brown, black, white, tan, pink, or pale.

Your color is a special gift from your family tree!

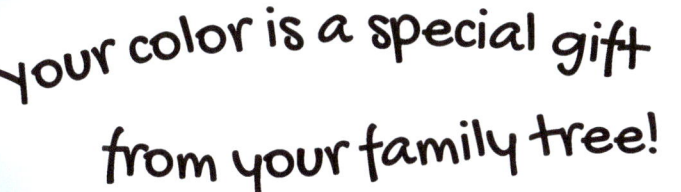

People might say your markings, stripes, freckles, spots, birthmarks, or scars are imperfections...

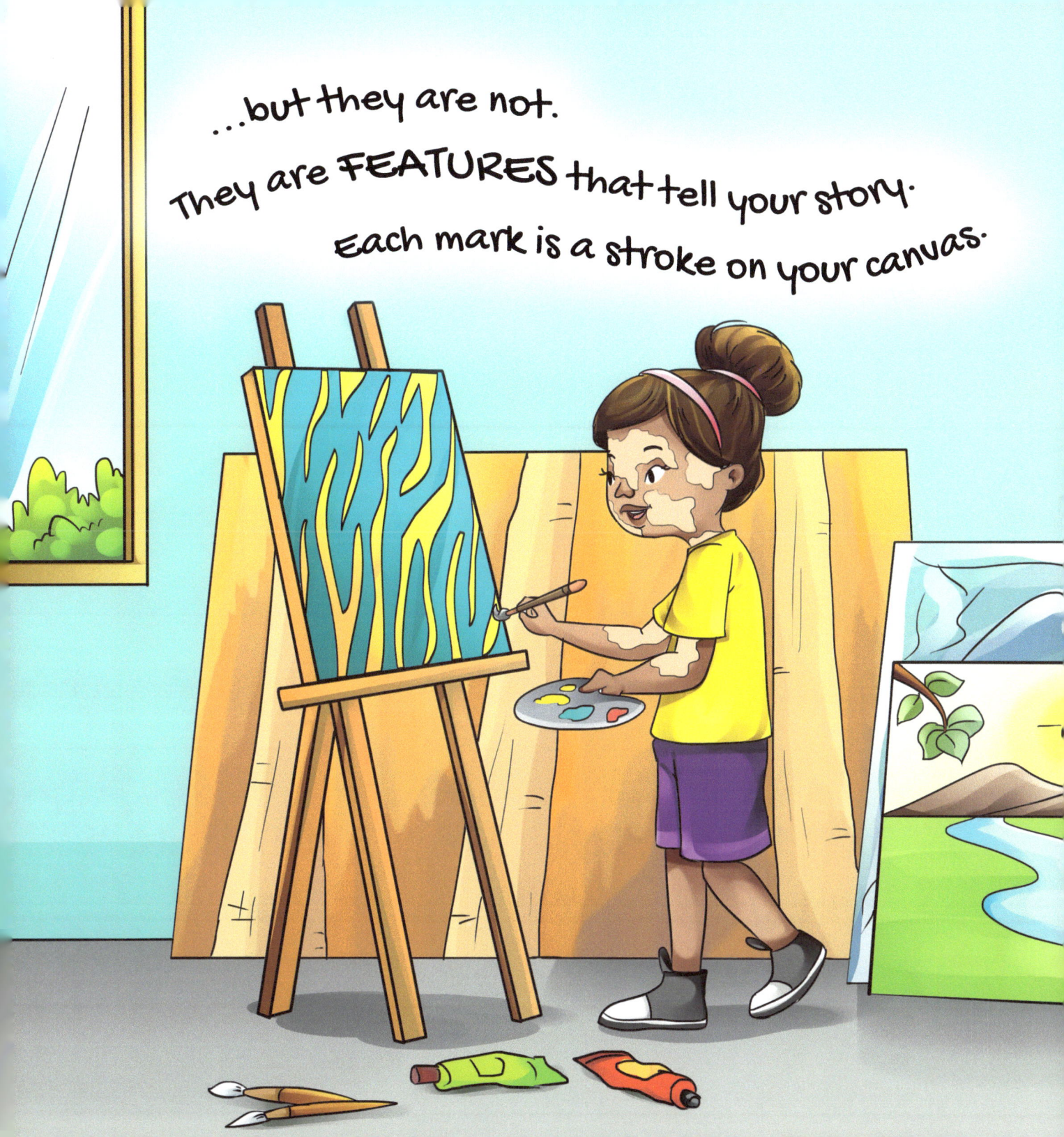

Your nose, any shape.

Your lips, full or thin.

Your ears, tiny or large.

All the parts of your face are a part of your identity.

It's good to be thankful for all it does.

Your beauty is not always found in your looks, it can be found in the way you treat others.

Your best features are the things that come from the inside! Kindness, empathy, compassion are what make you truly glow!

Your story needs to be shared whether it comes out shaky or bold, soft or loud.
Lisps, accents, and stutters might make us sound different, but it really doesn't matter.
Speak up, even when you fear the crowd.
Your voice matters! You are meant to be heard.
Sing loud, sign proud, speak out.
That's your IDENTITY!

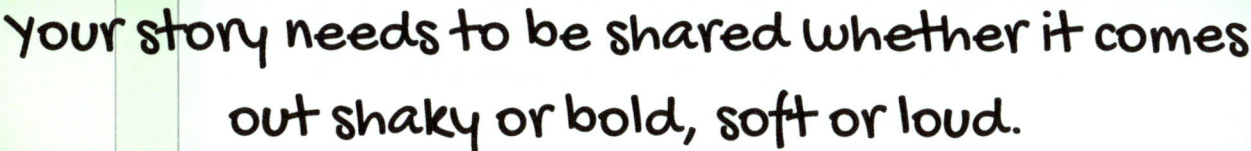

Your features should be celebrated, not fixed, and not changed. Stand up, stand out.

Embracing your features can change the world. It teaches others that it's okay to be themselves, too. Just like you. You are enough.

You are worthy.

Exactly as you are.

So say it LOUDLY and shout it out PROUDLY.

CHRISTINA TESTUT

I wrote this book to help change the narrative around body image. Every day I hear children, teenagers, and adults speaking poorly about themselves, whether in school, the supermarket, or social media. It is sad to listen to people referring to their features as flaws and to want to change or hide them. My goal for this book is for parents and children to learn to accept themselves as they are. I hope teachers bring this message into their classrooms so all students feel included and know that they matter, no matter what they look like. Finally, I want anyone struggling with poor body image, at any age, any gender, and any race, to pick this book up and be reminded that they are enough and worthy exactly the way they are.

Share this message with friends. Help spread EMBRACE YOUR FEATURES far and wide.

www.ingramcontent.com/pod-product-compliance
Lightning Source LLC
LaVergne TN
LVHW071651060526
838200LV00029B/429